WEALTH WHISPER

SECRETS OF ABUNDANCE

CHRIS JOSH

Copyright © 2024 by Chris Josh

TABLE OF CONTENT

INTRODUCTION

"Welcome to the world of abundance, where the whispers of wealth beckon you towards prosperity and fulfillment. In 'Wealth Whisper: Secrets of Abundance,' we embark on a transformative journey that transcends mere financial success, delving into the profound realms of abundance in all its forms.

In this book, I invite you to explore the hidden dimensions of wealth, not merely as a sum of material possessions, but as a state of being that encompasses richness in relationships, health, knowledge, and spiritual fulfillment. Drawing upon ancient wisdom, modern psychology, and personal experiences, 'Wealth Whisper unveils the timeless secrets that pave the path to abundance in every aspect of life.

In a world often fixated on scarcity and lack, this book serves as a guiding light, illuminating the abundance that surrounds us and empowering you to unlock its boundless potential. Whether you're seeking financial freedom, deeper connections, or a greater sense of purpose, the principles shared within these pages will inspire and equip you to manifest your desires with clarity and confidence.

Through insightful narratives, practical exercises, and thought-provoking reflections, 'Wealth Whisper' offers a roadmap to navigate the intricate landscape of abundance, helping you cultivate a mindset of prosperity and abundance consciousness. You'll learn to harness the power of gratitude, leverage the law of attraction, and embrace abundance as your birthright, enabling you to attract wealth and opportunities effortlessly.

Moreover, 'Wealth Whisper' transcends individual gain, emphasizing the importance of contributing to the collective well-being and fostering a ripple effect of abundance in the world. As you immerse yourself in these pages, prepare to embark on a transformative odyssey that will elevate your consciousness, expand your possibilities, and unveil the infinite wealth that resides within you.

So, heed the whispers of wealth, and let 'Wealth Whisper: Secrets of Abundance' be your companion on the journey towards a life of profound richness and fulfillment."

CHAPTER 1: UNVEILING THE NATURE OF ABUNDANCE

Welcome to the foundational exploration of abundance—the gateway to unlocking the boundless riches that await you. In this chapter, we embark on a profound journey of discovery, peeling back the layers of perception to reveal the true essence of abundance in its myriad forms.

In a world often clouded by notions of scarcity and lack, it's imperative to pause and reevaluate our understanding of abundance. Beyond the confines of material wealth lies a vast landscape of richness waiting to be explored—a tapestry woven with threads of love, joy, health, and fulfillment.

Our journey begins with a fundamental shift in perspective, transcending the narrow confines of conventional wisdom to embrace a holistic view of abundance. We'll delve into the multidimensional nature of abundance, recognizing it not merely as the accumulation of possessions, but as a state of being that permeates every aspect of our lives.

By unraveling the myths and misconceptions surrounding abundance, we pave the way for a deeper understanding of its inherent presence in the fabric of existence. Through introspection and inquiry, we uncover the limitless potential that resides within each of us, awaiting activation and expression.

Furthermore, we challenge the prevailing mindset of scarcity that pervades society, recognizing it as a barrier to experiencing the true abundance that surrounds us. With open hearts and minds, we embrace abundance consciousness—a paradigm shift that empowers us to attract wealth and opportunities effortlessly.

As we embark on this transformative exploration, I invite you to set aside preconceived notions and open yourself to the possibility of a life filled with abundance in all its forms. Prepare to be inspired, challenged, and ultimately liberated as we unveil the nature of abundance and embark on a journey towards a life of profound richness and fulfillment.

- Exploring the multidimensional facets of abundance

Abundance is a concept that extends far beyond the mere accumulation of material wealth. It encompasses a multitude of dimensions that collectively contribute to a rich and fulfilling life. Understanding the multidimensional facets of abundance involves recognizing and cultivating various aspects of well-being, each of which plays a vital role in fostering a sense of richness and fulfillment. Here, we delve into some of these dimensions:

1. **Material Abundance**: This dimension of abundance is perhaps the most familiar, relating to financial wealth and material possessions. It involves having the resources necessary to meet one's needs and desires comfortably. Material abundance provides the means to enjoy a certain standard of living, affording opportunities for comfort, security, and enjoyment of life's pleasures.

2. **Health and Vitality**: True abundance encompasses physical and mental well-being. Health is wealth, as the saying goes, and having vibrant health allows individuals to fully engage in life's experiences. Physical vitality, mental clarity, and emotional resilience are essential components of abundance in this dimension.

3. **Relationships and Connections**: Abundance extends to the realm of relationships and social connections. Meaningful connections with friends, family, and community members enrich our lives immeasurably. Strong, supportive relationships provide a sense of belonging, love, and

companionship, contributing to emotional well-being and overall life satisfaction.

4. **Personal Growth and Development**: Abundance includes opportunities for personal growth, learning, and self-improvement. Engaging in activities that expand knowledge, develop skills, and foster personal growth enriches life experiences and opens doors to new possibilities. Embracing challenges, pursuing passions, and cultivating resilience are integral aspects of abundance in this dimension.

5. **Spirituality and Purpose**: A sense of spiritual abundance involves feeling connected to something greater than oneself and experiencing a deep sense of purpose and meaning in life. This dimension encompasses spiritual practices, mindfulness, and a sense of alignment with one's values and beliefs. Cultivating spiritual abundance fosters inner peace, contentment, and a profound sense of fulfillment.

6. **Gratitude and Appreciation**: Gratitude is a cornerstone of abundance, involving the recognition

and appreciation of life's blessings, both big and small. Cultivating a mindset of gratitude enhances awareness of abundance in all its forms and fosters a sense of contentment and satisfaction with life.

7. **Creativity and Expression**: Abundance includes the freedom to express creativity and pursue passions. Engaging in creative endeavors, whether through art, music, writing, or other forms of expression, fosters a sense of joy, fulfillment, and self-expression.

8. **Contribution and Service**: True abundance involves giving back and making a positive impact on others and the world. Contributing to the well-being of others through acts of kindness, generosity, and service enhances feelings of abundance and fulfillment, creating a ripple effect of positivity and goodwill.

In summary, abundance encompasses a rich tapestry of dimensions that collectively contribute to a fulfilling and meaningful life. By nurturing and cultivating these various aspects of abundance, individuals can experience a profound sense of richness, fulfillment, and well-being in all areas of their lives.

- Understanding abundance as a state of being

Abundance as a state of being transcends mere material possessions or external circumstances. It is a profound inner experience characterized by a deep sense of fulfillment, contentment, and gratitude that arises from conscious recognition of the richness and infinite potential inherent in life. This state of being is cultivated through a shift in mindset, perception, and consciousness, allowing individuals to tap into the limitless abundance that exists within and around them. Here's a comprehensive discussion on abundance as a state of being:

1. **Mindset Shift**: Abundance as a state of being begins with a fundamental shift in mindset. It involves moving away from a mentality of scarcity, lack, and limitation towards one of abundance, possibility, and expansion. This shift involves reprogramming ingrained beliefs and thought patterns that reinforce scarcity thinking and embracing a perspective that focuses on abundance and opportunity.

2. **Gratitude and Appreciation**: Central to the state of abundance is the practice of gratitude and appreciation. Cultivating an attitude of gratitude involves consciously acknowledging and appreciating the abundance that already exists in one's life, whether it be in the form of relationships, opportunities, or simple everyday blessings. By shifting focus towards gratitude, individuals amplify their awareness of abundance and attract more of it into their lives.

3. **Presence and Awareness**: Abundance is experienced in the present moment through a deep sense of awareness and presence. By fully

immersing oneself in the present moment, individuals can connect with the richness of life unfolding around them and experience a profound sense of abundance in the here and now. Mindfulness practices such as meditation, deep breathing, and conscious awareness facilitate this state of being.

4. **Alignment with Purpose**: True abundance arises from living in alignment with one's purpose and values. When individuals are engaged in activities that resonate with their authentic selves and contribute to the greater good, they experience a sense of fulfillment and abundance that goes beyond material wealth. Aligning actions with purpose creates a sense of flow and harmony, enabling individuals to tap into their innate potential and creativity.

5. **Generosity and Contribution**: Abundance as a state of being is not solely focused on personal gain but also involves giving back and making a positive impact on others. Acts of generosity, kindness, and service not only benefit those on the receiving end

but also foster a deep sense of fulfillment and abundance within the giver. By sharing one's time, talents, and resources with others, individuals amplify the abundance in their lives and contribute to the collective well-being of humanity.

6. **Emotional Resilience and Inner Peace**: Abundance is characterized by emotional resilience and inner peace, even in the face of challenges and adversity. Individuals who embody abundance as a state of being can maintain a sense of calm and equanimity amidst life's ups and downs, knowing that they possess the inner resources to navigate any situation with grace and resilience.

7. **Connection to the Divine or Higher Self**: For many, abundance as a state of being involves a spiritual dimension, whether it be through connection to a higher power, the universe, or one's higher self. This spiritual connection provides a sense of guidance, purpose, and support, anchoring individuals in a deep sense of trust and faith in the inherent abundance of the universe.

In essence, abundance as a state of being is a holistic and transformative experience that transcends external circumstances and originates from within. By cultivating a mindset of abundance, practicing gratitude, living in alignment with purpose, and embodying generosity and resilience, individuals can tap into the boundless richness of life and experience a profound sense of fulfillment, joy, and contentment in every moment.

- Challenging scarcity mindset and embracing abundance consciousness

Challenging a scarcity mindset and embracing abundance consciousness is a transformative process that involves shifting ingrained beliefs, thought patterns, and behaviors. It requires a deliberate effort to reframe perceptions, cultivate gratitude, and adopt a mindset that focuses on abundance, possibility, and prosperity. Here's a comprehensive discussion of the process:

1. **Awareness:** The first step in challenging a scarcity mindset is becoming aware of its presence in one's life. This involves recognizing how scarcity thinking manifests, such as feelings of fear, lack, and limitation, and identifying the underlying beliefs and thought patterns that contribute to this mindset.

2. **Identification of Scarcity Beliefs**: Once awareness is established, individuals can identify specific scarcity beliefs that are holding them back. These beliefs may include thoughts such as "there's never enough," "I'll never be successful," or "I don't deserve abundance." By shining a light on these beliefs, individuals can begin to challenge their validity and explore alternative perspectives.

3. **Cognitive Reframing**: Challenging a scarcity mindset requires consciously reframing negative thoughts and beliefs into more empowering ones. This involves questioning the accuracy of scarcity-

based thinking and replacing it with thoughts that align with abundance and possibility. For example, reframing "there's never enough" to "there is abundance all around me, and I attract wealth effortlessly."

4. **Gratitude Practice:** Cultivating a practice of gratitude is essential for shifting from scarcity to abundance consciousness. Regularly acknowledging and appreciating the abundance that already exists in one's life helps to rewire the brain for positivity and abundance. Keeping a gratitude journal, expressing thanks for small blessings, and focusing on abundance rather than lack are effective ways to cultivate gratitude.

5. **Visualization and Affirmations**: Visualization and affirmations are powerful tools for reprogramming the subconscious mind and reinforcing abundance consciousness. Engaging in visualization exercises where one imagines living a life of abundance in vivid detail helps to imprint positive images and beliefs into the subconscious. Affirmations—positive statements that affirm

abundance and prosperity—can also be repeated daily to reinforce a mindset of abundance.

6. **Surrounding Oneself with Abundance**: Surrounding oneself with people, resources, and environments that embody abundance can help reinforce abundance consciousness. Associating with individuals who have a positive mindset, investing time in personal development activities, and exposing oneself to inspirational content are all ways to immerse oneself in an abundance mindset.

7. **Taking Inspired Action**: Embracing abundance consciousness involves taking inspired action towards one's goals and desires. Rather than operating from a place of fear and scarcity, individuals with abundance consciousness approach challenges with confidence, knowing that opportunities are abundant and success is within reach. Taking consistent, aligned action towards goals reinforces belief in one's ability to manifest abundance.

8. **Embracing a Growth Mindset**: Finally, embracing a growth mindset is integral to maintaining abundance consciousness. Viewing challenges as opportunities for growth, learning from setbacks, and remaining open to new possibilities fosters a mindset of abundance and resilience.

In summary, challenging a scarcity mindset and embracing abundance consciousness is a multifaceted process that involves awareness, identification of limiting beliefs, cognitive reframing, and gratitude practice, visualization, surrounding oneself with abundance, taking inspired action, and embracing a growth mindset. Through consistent practice and commitment, individuals can shift from a mindset of scarcity to one of abundance, unlocking their full potential for prosperity and fulfillment.

CHAPTER 2: THE POWER OF PERCEPTION: SHIFTING YOUR MINDSET

Welcome to the transformative exploration of perception and mindset—the keys to unlocking the boundless potential of abundance in your life. In this chapter, we delve into the profound influence of perception on our experiences, beliefs, and ultimately, our reality. By understanding the power of perception and learning to shift our mindset, we gain the ability to shape our lives in alignment with abundance and possibility.

At the heart of this chapter lies the recognition that our thoughts and beliefs shape our experiences and outcomes. The lens through which we view the world—our perception—determines whether we see scarcity or abundance, limitation or opportunity. By harnessing the power of perception and consciously choosing to adopt a mindset of abundance, we can transform our reality and create a life filled with richness, fulfillment, and prosperity.

Throughout this chapter, we will explore the intricate interplay between perception, mindset, and abundance consciousness. We'll uncover the underlying beliefs and thought patterns that contribute to scarcity thinking and examine the profound impact they have on our lives. Moreover, we'll delve into practical strategies and techniques for shifting our mindset towards abundance, empowering ourselves to manifest our desires with clarity and confidence.

Central to our exploration is the understanding that mindset is not fixed but rather malleable—a product of conditioning, beliefs, and experiences that can be consciously shifted and reprogrammed. By challenging limiting beliefs, reframing negative thought patterns, and cultivating a mindset of possibility and abundance, we open ourselves to a world of infinite opportunities and potential.

Furthermore, we'll explore the role of gratitude, visualization, and affirmations in shaping perception and reinforcing abundance consciousness. These powerful practices serve as catalysts for transformation, helping to rewire the brain for positivity and abundance, and aligning us with the flow of universal abundance.

As we embark on this journey of perception and mindset, I invite you to approach with an open mind and a willingness to explore new possibilities. Prepare to challenge your existing beliefs, expand your awareness, and unlock the transformative power of perception in your quest for abundance and fulfillment. Together, let us embark on a journey of discovery and empowerment, as we harness the inherent power of perception to shape our reality and create a life of abundance beyond measure.

- Identifying limiting beliefs and scarcity programming

Identifying limiting beliefs and scarcity programming is a crucial step in the journey towards abundance consciousness and personal growth. These beliefs are deeply ingrained thought patterns and perceptions that hinder individuals from realizing their full potential and experiencing true abundance in their lives. The process of identifying these beliefs involves introspection, self-awareness, and a willingness to confront and challenge deeply held assumptions about oneself and the world. Here's a comprehensive discussion of the process:

1. **Self-Reflection and Introspection**: The first step in identifying limiting beliefs and scarcity programming is to engage in self-reflection and introspection. This involves setting aside time for quiet contemplation and examining one's thoughts,

feelings, and behaviors. Journaling, meditation, and mindfulness practices can be helpful tools for gaining insight into the subconscious mind and uncovering hidden beliefs.

2. **Exploring Core Beliefs**: Core beliefs are deeply ingrained convictions about oneself, others, and the world that shape perception and behavior. Identifying limiting beliefs requires examining these core beliefs and questioning their validity. Common examples of limiting beliefs include "I'm not good enough," "Money is scarce," or "Success is only for others." By identifying the core beliefs that underlie these statements, individuals can begin to unravel the patterns of scarcity thinking.

3. **Recognizing Patterns and Triggers**: Limiting beliefs often manifest as recurring patterns of thought and behavior, triggered by specific situations or events. By paying attention to these patterns and observing the situations that trigger them, individuals can gain insight into their underlying beliefs. Keeping a journal or making

notes of recurring thoughts and emotions can help in identifying patterns and triggers.

4. **Examining Childhood Conditioning**: Many limiting beliefs and scarcity programming originate from childhood experiences and conditioning. Messages received from parents, teachers, and society can shape beliefs about worthiness, success, and abundance. By reflecting on childhood experiences and examining the messages received during formative years, individuals can uncover the roots of their limiting beliefs and begin to challenge them.

5. **Seeking Feedback and Perspective**: Sometimes, it can be challenging to identify our own limiting beliefs due to their deeply ingrained nature. Seeking feedback from trusted friends, mentors, or therapists can provide valuable perspective and insight. Others may be able to observe patterns and beliefs that are not immediately apparent to us, helping us to identify and address them more effectively.

6. **Questioning Assumptions and Beliefs**:
Challenging limiting beliefs involves questioning
the assumptions and beliefs that underlie them. This
process requires critical thinking and a willingness
to challenge the status quo. Asking questions such
as "Is this belief true?" "Where did this belief come
from?" and "How does this belief serve me?" can
help individuals gain clarity and perspective on
their limiting beliefs.

7. **Exploring the Evidence**: Another effective
strategy for identifying limiting beliefs is to
examine the evidence that supports or contradicts
them. Often, individuals hold onto beliefs that are
not supported by objective evidence or personal
experience. By critically evaluating the evidence for
and against a belief, individuals can gain a more
balanced perspective and begin to challenge beliefs
that no longer serve them.

8. **Seeking Professional Help**: In some cases,
identifying and addressing limiting beliefs may
require the support of a professional therapist or
coach. These professionals are trained to help

individuals explore their beliefs, challenge negative thought patterns, and develop more empowering perspectives. Seeking professional help can provide additional guidance and support in the process of identifying and overcoming limiting beliefs.

In summary, identifying limiting beliefs and scarcity programming is a transformative process that requires self-reflection, introspection, and a willingness to question deeply held assumptions. By examining core beliefs, recognizing patterns and triggers, exploring childhood conditioning, seeking feedback, questioning assumptions, exploring the evidence, and seeking professional help when needed, individuals can begin to unravel the layers of scarcity thinking and move towards a mindset of abundance and possibility.

- Cultivating a mindset of prosperity and abundance

Cultivating a mindset of prosperity and abundance is a transformative process that involves shifting one's beliefs, thoughts, and attitudes towards wealth, success, and fulfillment. This process requires intentional effort, self-awareness, and a willingness to challenge ingrained patterns of scarcity thinking. Here's a comprehensive discussion on the process:

1. **Awareness and Recognition:** The first step in cultivating a mindset of prosperity and abundance is becoming aware of one's current mindset and recognizing any patterns of scarcity thinking that may be present. This involves observing one's thoughts, beliefs, and attitudes towards money, success, and abundance.

2. **Challenging Limiting Beliefs:** Limiting beliefs are often at the root of scarcity thinking and can hinder the cultivation of abundance consciousness. Identifying and challenging these beliefs is essential for creating space for prosperity to flow. This process involves questioning the validity of limiting beliefs and reframing them into more empowering beliefs that support abundance.

3. **Gratitude Practice:** Gratitude is a powerful tool for shifting from scarcity to abundance consciousness. Cultivating a daily practice of gratitude involves acknowledging and appreciating the abundance that already exists in one's life, whether it be in the form of relationships, opportunities, or simple blessings. Practicing gratitude helps to rewire the brain for positivity and abundance, making room for more blessings to flow into one's life.

4. **Positive Visualization:** Visualization is another effective technique for cultivating a mindset of prosperity and abundance. By visualizing oneself living a life of abundance in vivid detail, individuals

can imprint positive images and beliefs into their subconscious mind. This process helps to create a mental blueprint for success and aligns one's thoughts and actions with their desired outcomes.

5. Affirmations and Positive Self-Talk: Affirmations are positive statements that affirm one's desired reality. Incorporating affirmations into daily practice can help to reprogram the subconscious mind for abundance and success. By repeating affirmations that align with abundance consciousness, individuals can reinforce positive beliefs and attitudes towards wealth and prosperity.

6. Embracing a Growth Mindset: A growth mindset is essential for cultivating a mindset of prosperity and abundance. Embracing the belief that one's abilities and intelligence can be developed through effort and persistence opens the door to infinite possibilities and potential. Individuals with a growth mindset view challenges as opportunities for growth and learning, rather than obstacles to be avoided.

7. **Taking Inspired Action**: Cultivating a mindset of prosperity and abundance involves taking inspired action towards one's goals and desires. Rather than waiting for success to happen, individuals with abundance consciousness take proactive steps to create the life they desire. Taking consistent, aligned action towards goals reinforces belief in one's ability to manifest abundance and attracts opportunities for success.

8. **Surrounding Oneself with Abundance:** Surrounding oneself with people, resources, and environments that embody abundance is essential for cultivating an abundance mindset. Associating with individuals who have a positive mindset, investing time in personal development activities, and exposing oneself to inspirational content can help to immerse oneself in an abundance mindset.

9. **Practicing Generosity:** Finally, practicing generosity and giving back to others is a powerful way to cultivate a mindset of prosperity and abundance. By sharing one's time, talents, and resources with others, individuals tap into the flow

of abundance and create a ripple effect of positivity and goodwill.

In summary, cultivating a mindset of prosperity and abundance is a holistic process that involves awareness, gratitude, and positive visualization, affirmations, embracing a growth mindset, taking inspired action, surrounding oneself with abundance, and practicing generosity. By committing to this transformative process, individuals can unlock their full potential, attract greater abundance into their lives, and create a life of fulfillment and prosperity.

- Harnessing the law of attraction to manifest abundance

Harnessing the Law of Attraction to manifest abundance is a process rooted in the belief that like attracts like—meaning, the energy you put out into the universe attracts similar energy back to you.

This concept has gained popularity in recent years, particularly in the realm of personal development and manifestation. Here's a comprehensive discussion of the process:

1. **Understanding the Law of Attraction**: The Law of Attraction is based on the principle that thoughts, beliefs, and feelings have the power to shape reality. According to this law, whatever you focus on consistently—whether positive or negative—will manifest in your life. Understanding the fundamentals of the Law of Attraction is essential for effectively harnessing its power to manifest abundance.

2. **Clarifying Intentions and Desires**: The first step in manifesting abundance through the Law of Attraction is clarifying your intentions and desires. This involves getting clear about what you want to attract into your life, whether it be financial wealth, fulfilling relationships, vibrant health, or personal growth. Writing down your intentions and visualizing them as already achieved helps to clarify and amplify your desires.

3. Cultivating Positive Thoughts and Beliefs:
Cultivating a positive mindset is essential for harnessing the Law of Attraction. This involves consciously choosing to focus on thoughts and beliefs that align with abundance and prosperity, rather than scarcity and lack. Affirmations, visualization, and gratitude practice are effective techniques for shifting to a positive mindset and reprogramming the subconscious mind for abundance.

4. Visualizing Abundance: Visualization is a powerful tool for manifesting abundance through the Law of Attraction. By vividly imagining yourself already in possession of the abundance you desire, you send a clear signal to the universe about your intentions. Visualization helps to align your thoughts, feelings, and actions with your desires, making it more likely for them to manifest in reality.

5. **Practicing Gratitude:** Gratitude is a key component of the Law of Attraction. Expressing gratitude for the abundance already present in your life—whether it be relationships, opportunities, or simple blessings—helps to raise your vibration and attract more abundance into your life. Keeping a gratitude journal, expressing thanks daily, and focusing on the positive aspects of your life are effective ways to cultivate gratitude.

6. **Setting Intentions and Taking Inspired Action:** Setting clear intentions and taking inspired action is essential for manifesting abundance through the Law of Attraction. While the Law of Attraction emphasizes the power of thought and belief, it also requires taking practical steps towards your goals. By aligning your actions with your intentions and staying open to opportunities, you create momentum and move closer to manifesting your desires.

7. **Letting Go of Attachment:** Letting go of attachment to outcomes is another important aspect of harnessing the Law of Attraction. While it's important to set clear intentions and take inspired action, it's equally important to release attachment to how and when your desires will manifest. Trusting in the process and surrendering to the universe's timing allows for greater flow and abundance to enter your life.

8. **Maintaining a Positive Vibration:** Your vibration—your energetic frequency—plays a crucial role in manifesting abundance through the Law of Attraction. Maintaining a positive vibration involves surrounding yourself with positivity, engaging in activities that bring you joy and fulfillment, and avoiding negativity as much as possible. By raising your vibration, you become a magnet for abundance and attract more of what you desire into your life.

9. **Practicing Patience and Persistence:** Manifesting abundance through the Law of Attraction is not always instantaneous, and it

requires patience and persistence. Trusting in the process, staying committed to your intentions, and remaining open to the possibilities are key to success. Even when faced with challenges or setbacks, maintaining a positive mindset and continuing to take inspired action can lead to eventual manifestation.

In summary, harnessing the Law of Attraction to manifest abundance involves understanding the principles of the Law of Attraction, clarifying intentions and desires, cultivating positive thoughts and beliefs, visualizing abundance, practicing gratitude, setting intentions and taking inspired action, letting go of attachment, maintaining a positive vibration, and practicing patience and persistence. By incorporating these practices into your daily life, you can harness the power of the Law of Attraction to attract greater abundance, fulfillment, and success into your life.

CHAPTER 3: GRATITUDE: THE GATEWAY TO ABUNDANCE

Welcome to a profound exploration of gratitude—the transformative force that serves as the gateway to abundance in all areas of life. In this chapter, we embark on a journey of deep reflection and appreciation, uncovering the immense power of gratitude to elevate our consciousness, enrich our experiences, and attract greater abundance into our lives.

Gratitude is more than just a fleeting emotion or polite gesture; it is a fundamental attitude and way of being that shapes our perception of the world. It involves acknowledging and appreciating the blessings, opportunities, and gifts that surround us each day, no matter how small or seemingly insignificant.

At its core, gratitude is about recognizing the abundance that already exists in our lives, even amidst challenges and adversity. It is a shift in perspective—a lens through which we view the world with awe, wonder, and appreciation for the richness of life's experiences.

In this chapter, we will explore the profound effects of gratitude on our physical, emotional, and spiritual well-being. We'll uncover the science behind gratitude and its profound impact on brain chemistry, immune function, and overall health. Moreover, we'll delve into the transformative power of gratitude to shift our vibration and attract greater abundance into our lives.

Through practical exercises, reflection prompts, and real-life examples, we'll learn how to cultivate a daily practice of gratitude that becomes a natural and integral part of our lives. From keeping a gratitude journal to expressing thanks in moments of joy and adversity, we'll discover how simple acts of gratitude can transform our reality and open the floodgates to abundance.

Furthermore, we'll explore the concept of radical gratitude—a profound shift towards unconditional appreciation and acceptance of all that life has to offer. By embracing radical gratitude, we release resistance, let go of attachments, and surrender to the flow of abundance that surrounds us.

As we journey deeper into the heart of gratitude, I invite you to open your heart and mind to the transformative power of this practice. Prepare to be inspired, uplifted, and profoundly changed as we explore gratitude as the gateway to abundance and embark on a journey of profound richness, fulfillment, and joy.

- Understanding the transformative power of gratitude

The transformative power of gratitude extends far beyond mere expressions of thanks; it encompasses a profound shift in mindset and perspective that can profoundly impact every aspect of our lives. Here's a comprehensive discussion on the transformative power of gratitude:

1. **Shift in Perspective**: Gratitude involves shifting from a mindset of scarcity and lack to one of abundance and appreciation. By focusing on the blessings, opportunities, and gifts that surround us, even in challenging times, gratitude helps us see the world through a lens of positivity and abundance.

2. **Enhanced Emotional Well-being:** Practicing gratitude has been linked to increased levels of happiness, joy, and overall well-being. When we express gratitude, our brains release

neurotransmitters such as dopamine and serotonin, often referred to as "feel-good" chemicals, which can uplift our mood and promote emotional resilience.

3. Improved Physical Health: Gratitude has been shown to have numerous physical health benefits, including reduced stress levels, lower blood pressure, and improved immune function. By reducing the body's stress response and promoting relaxation, gratitude can contribute to better overall health and longevity.

4. Stronger Relationships: Gratitude strengthens relationships by fostering feelings of appreciation, connection, and reciprocity. When we express gratitude towards others, whether through words, actions, or gestures, we deepen our bonds and create a positive feedback loop of kindness and generosity.

5. Increased Resilience: Gratitude cultivates resilience by helping us reframe challenges and setbacks as opportunities for growth and learning. Rather than dwelling on difficulties, gratitude encourages us to focus on the lessons and silver linings that emerge from adversity, empowering us to bounce back stronger than before.

6. **Heightened Mindfulness and Presence:** Practicing gratitude fosters mindfulness and presence by grounding us in the present moment and increasing our awareness of the beauty and abundance that surrounds us. By cultivating a habit of noticing and appreciating the small wonders of life, we become more attuned to the richness of each moment.

7. **Greater Sense of Purpose and Meaning:** Gratitude deepens our sense of purpose and meaning by helping us recognize the interconnectedness of all things and our place in the universe. When we express gratitude for the people, experiences, and opportunities that have shaped us, we gain a deeper understanding of our values, goals, and aspirations.

8. **Manifestation of Abundance**: Gratitude is a powerful tool for manifesting abundance and

attracting more of what we desire into our lives. By focusing on what we are grateful for, we send a clear signal to the universe that we are open to receiving more blessings and opportunities, creating a positive feedback loop of abundance.

9. **Cultivation of Radical Acceptance**: Radical acceptance, or unconditional acceptance of what is, is a core aspect of gratitude practice. By embracing all aspects of our lives with gratitude, including both the joys and the challenges, we cultivate a sense of peace, contentment, and surrender to the flow of life.

In summary, the transformative power of gratitude lies in its ability to shift our perspective, enhance our well-being, strengthen our relationships, increase our resilience, deepen our sense of purpose and meaning, manifest abundance, and cultivate radical acceptance. By making gratitude a daily practice, we can unlock its profound potential to transform our lives and create a reality filled with joy, abundance, and fulfillment.

- Practicing daily gratitude rituals to amplify abundance

Practicing daily gratitude rituals is a powerful way to amplify abundance in our lives. These rituals involve intentional actions and exercises designed to cultivate a mindset of appreciation and abundance. Here's a comprehensive discussion on the process:

1. **Morning Gratitude Practice:** Starting the day with a gratitude ritual sets a positive tone and mindset for the day ahead. Upon waking, take a few moments to reflect on three things you are grateful for. These could be simple blessings like the warmth of the sun, the love of family, or the opportunity to pursue your passions. By focusing on the positive aspects of your life from the moment you wake up, you set the stage for a day filled with abundance.

2. **Gratitude Journaling:** Keeping a gratitude journal is a popular and effective daily ritual for amplifying abundance. Set aside time each day to write down three to five things you are grateful for. Reflect on both the big blessings and the small joys that you experienced throughout the day. Writing down your blessings not only helps you acknowledge them but also reinforces a mindset of gratitude and abundance.

3. **Expressing Gratitude to Others:** Expressing gratitude to others is a powerful way to amplify abundance in your relationships. Make it a daily practice to express appreciation to at least one person in your life. This could be a family member, friend, colleague, or even a stranger who has made a positive impact on your day. Whether through a heartfelt thank-you note, a kind gesture, or a simple word of appreciation, expressing gratitude strengthens your connections and fosters a culture of abundance.

4. **Mindful Gratitude Meditation:** Incorporating mindfulness meditation into your daily routine can

deepen your gratitude practice and amplify its effects. Set aside time each day to practice a gratitude meditation, focusing on the sensations of gratitude in your body and the emotions of appreciation in your heart. Allow yourself to fully immerse in the feeling of gratitude, cultivating a sense of abundance and well-being.

5. Gratitude Walks or Nature Immersion: Spending time in nature and immersing yourself in its beauty is a powerful way to cultivate gratitude and amplify abundance. Take a daily gratitude walk in nature, focusing on the sights, sounds, and sensations around you. Notice the beauty of the natural world, the abundance of life teeming around you, and the interconnectedness of all living things. Allow yourself to feel a sense of awe and appreciation for the abundance of nature and its gifts.

6. Gratitude Visualization: Visualization is a potent tool for amplifying abundance through gratitude. Incorporate a daily visualization practice into your routine, where you visualize yourself surrounded by abundance in all areas of your life. Imagine your goals and desires already achieved, feeling the emotions of gratitude and fulfillment as if they were already a reality. Visualization helps to program your subconscious mind for abundance, aligning your thoughts and actions with your desires.

7. **Evening Reflection and Gratitude:** End each day with a reflection on the blessings and abundance that unfolded throughout the day. Before going to bed, take a few moments to review your day and identify three things you are grateful for. Reflect on the positive experiences, lessons learned, and moments of joy that you experienced. By ending the day with a mindset of gratitude, you reinforce the abundance mindset and set the stage for a restful and rejuvenating night's sleep.

In summary, practicing daily gratitude rituals involves incorporating intentional actions and exercises into your daily routine to cultivate a mindset of appreciation and abundance. By starting the day with gratitude, journaling your blessings, expressing appreciation to others, practicing mindful meditation, immersing yourself in nature, visualizing abundance, and reflecting on your blessings each evening, you amplify abundance in all areas of your life and create a reality filled with joy, fulfillment, and gratitude.

- Cultivating an attitude of appreciation towards life's blessings

Cultivating an attitude of appreciation towards life's blessings is a transformative process that involves consciously shifting your mindset to focus on the positive aspects of your life. It requires cultivating a sense of gratitude and appreciation for the abundance that surrounds you, no matter how big or small. Here's a comprehensive discussion of the process:

1. **Mindfulness and Presence:** Cultivating an attitude of appreciation begins with mindfulness and

presence. By being fully present at the moment, you become more aware of the beauty, joy, and blessings that exist in your life. Mindfulness practices such as meditation, deep breathing, and conscious awareness help to anchor you in the present moment and open your eyes to the abundance that surrounds you.

2. **Shift in Perspective:** Appreciation involves shifting your perspective from one of scarcity and lack to one of abundance and gratitude. Instead of focusing on what you lack or what's going wrong in your life, consciously choose to focus on what you have and what's going right. This shift in perspective allows you to see the blessings and opportunities that are already present in your life.

3. **Gratitude Journaling:** Keeping a gratitude journal is a powerful tool for cultivating an attitude of appreciation. Set aside time each day to write down three to five things you are grateful for. These could be simple blessings like a warm cup of tea, a kind gesture from a friend, or a beautiful sunset. By regularly acknowledging and appreciating the

blessings in your life, you train your mind to focus on the positive aspects of your reality.

4. **Counting Your Blessings:** Take time each day to count your blessings and reflect on the abundance in your life. This could involve mentally listing the things you are grateful for, such as your health, relationships, home, job, or talents. By consciously acknowledging and appreciating the blessings in your life, you create a sense of abundance and fulfillment.

5. **Practicing Random Acts of Kindness:** Engaging in acts of kindness towards others is another way to cultivate an attitude of appreciation. Whether it's offering a helping hand, giving a compliment, or performing a random act of kindness, expressing generosity and compassion towards others fosters a sense of gratitude and appreciation for the abundance of love and connection in your life.

6. **Embracing Imperfection and Growth:**

Appreciation involves embracing imperfection and seeing the beauty in life's challenges and setbacks. Instead of viewing obstacles as roadblocks, see them as opportunities for growth and learning. Embrace the journey of life with all its ups and downs, knowing that each experience contributes to your growth and evolution.

7. **Surrounding Yourself with Positivity:**

Surrounding yourself with positivity and inspiration is essential for cultivating an attitude of appreciation. Spend time with people who uplift and inspire you, engage in activities that bring you joy and fulfillment, and expose yourself to uplifting content such as books, podcasts, or music. By surrounding yourself with positivity, you create an environment that nourishes and reinforces your attitude of appreciation.

8. **Practicing Self-Compassion:** Lastly, practicing self-compassion is crucial for cultivating an attitude of appreciation. Treat yourself with kindness, compassion, and understanding, especially during

challenging times. Acknowledge your strengths, celebrate your accomplishments, and forgive yourself for any perceived shortcomings. By showing yourself the same love and appreciation you extend to others, you deepen your sense of gratitude and appreciation for the abundance of blessings in your life.

In summary, cultivating an attitude of appreciation towards life's blessings involves practicing mindfulness and presence, shifting your perspective from scarcity to abundance, keeping a gratitude journal, counting your blessings, practicing random acts of kindness, embracing imperfection and growth, surrounding yourself with positivity, and practicing self-compassion. By consciously choosing to focus on the positive aspects of your life and expressing gratitude for the abundance that surrounds you, you create a reality filled with joy, fulfillment, and appreciation.

CHAPTER 4: ATTRACTING WEALTH: STRATEGIES AND PRACTICES

Welcome to a transformative exploration of wealth attraction—an endeavor that goes beyond mere financial gain to encompass a holistic approach to abundance in all aspects of life. In this chapter, we delve into the strategies and practices that empower individuals to magnetize wealth and prosperity into their lives through alignment, intention, and action.

Attracting wealth is not just about amassing monetary riches; it's about creating a life of abundance, fulfillment, and purpose. It involves cultivating a mindset of abundance, leveraging the power of intention, and taking inspired action towards one's goals and aspirations.

In this chapter, we'll explore a range of strategies and practices for attracting wealth, drawing upon principles from psychology, spirituality, and personal development. From mindset shifts to practical action steps, we'll uncover the keys to unlocking financial abundance and living a life of prosperity.

Throughout this chapter, we'll examine the following key themes:

1. **Mindset Mastery:** Cultivating a mindset of abundance is the foundation for attracting wealth. We'll explore techniques for shifting limiting beliefs, cultivating a wealth mindset, and aligning your thoughts and beliefs with your financial goals.

2. **Intention Setting:** Setting clear intentions is essential for manifesting wealth. We'll discuss the power of intention setting and explore practical strategies for clarifying your financial goals and aligning your actions with your desires.

3. **Strategic Planning:** Developing a strategic plan is crucial for turning intentions into reality. We'll delve into strategies for creating a roadmap to financial success, setting SMART goals, and taking consistent action towards your objectives.

4. **Abundance Practices:** Engaging in daily abundance practices is key to attracting wealth. We'll explore rituals, habits, and routines that cultivate a sense of abundance and prosperity in your life, from gratitude practices to visualization techniques.

5. **Wealth Building Strategies:** Implementing wealth-building strategies is essential for achieving financial abundance. We'll discuss investment strategies, income generation tactics, and wealth accumulation techniques that empower you to build lasting prosperity.

6. **Leveraging the Law of Attraction:** Harnessing the Law of Attraction is a powerful tool for attracting wealth. We'll explore how to align your energy with abundance, overcome a scarcity

mindset, and magnetize wealth into your life through the power of intention and vibration.

7. **Giving Back:** Practicing generosity and giving back is a key component of attracting wealth. We'll discuss the importance of an abundance mindset, philanthropy, and making a positive impact in the world as integral aspects of wealth attraction.

As we embark on this journey of wealth attraction, I invite you to approach with an open mind and a willingness to explore new possibilities. By integrating these strategies and practices into your life, you'll empower yourself to attract greater abundance, prosperity, and fulfillment into every area of your life. Let's embark on this transformative journey together, as we unlock the secrets to attracting wealth and creating a life of abundance beyond measure.

- Setting clear intentions and goals for financial abundance

Setting clear intentions and goals for financial abundance is a crucial step in manifesting wealth and prosperity. It involves clarifying your desires, identifying specific objectives, and creating a roadmap for achieving financial success. Here's a comprehensive discussion of the process:

1. **Reflect on Your Values and Priorities:** Before setting financial intentions and goals, take time to reflect on your values, priorities, and long-term aspirations. Consider what truly matters to you and what you envision for your ideal life. This reflection helps ensure that your financial goals align with your broader vision and sense of purpose.

2. **Define Your Definition of Financial Abundance:** Financial abundance means different things to different people. Take some time to define

what financial abundance looks like for you. Is it having a certain amount of savings, achieving a specific income level, being debt-free, or having the freedom to pursue your passions without financial worry? Clarifying your definition of financial abundance provides a clear target to aim for.

3. **Set Specific, Measurable, Achievable, Relevant, and Time-Bound (SMART) Goals:** When setting financial intentions and goals, use the SMART criteria to ensure they are well-defined and actionable. Specific goals clearly outline what you want to achieve, measurable goals can be tracked and evaluated, achievable goals are realistic given your current circumstances, relevant goals align with your values and priorities, and time-bound goals have a deadline for completion.

4. **Break Down Larger Goals into Smaller Milestones:** If your financial goals are large or long-term, break them down into smaller, more manageable milestones. This makes them less overwhelming and allows you to track your progress more effectively. For example, if your goal

is to save $100,000, break it down into monthly or yearly savings targets.

5. **Visualize Your Goals and Affirm Them Daily:** Visualization is a powerful technique for manifesting financial abundance. Take time each day to visualize yourself already achieving your financial goals. Imagine what it feels like to have achieved your desired level of wealth and abundance. Additionally, affirm your goals daily by repeating positive affirmations that reinforce your belief in your ability to manifest financial abundance.

6. **Write Down Your Goals and Intentions:** Putting your financial goals and intentions in writing reinforces your commitment and increases the likelihood of success. Create a written statement or vision board that clearly articulates your financial goals and the specific outcomes you desire. Place this written documentation somewhere visible to serve as a constant reminder of your intentions.

7. **Create an Action Plan:** Once you've clarified your financial intentions and goals, create an action plan outlining the steps you need to take to achieve them. Break down each goal into actionable tasks and assign deadlines for completion. Having a clear plan of action helps you stay focused, organized, and motivated as you work towards financial abundance.

8. **Regularly Review and Adjust Your Goals:** Financial goals are not set in stone, and it's essential to review and adjust them periodically as circumstances change. Regularly evaluate your progress towards your goals, celebrate your achievements, and make any necessary adjustments to your action plan to keep yourself on track.

9. **Stay Committed and Persistent:** Achieving financial abundance requires commitment, persistence, and resilience. Stay focused on your goals, even when faced with challenges or setbacks. Trust in the process, stay adaptable and maintain a positive mindset as you work towards manifesting your financial aspirations.

In summary, setting clear intentions and goals for financial abundance involves reflecting on your values, defining your definition of financial abundance, setting SMART goals, breaking down larger goals into smaller milestones, visualizing your goals, writing them down, creating an action plan, regularly reviewing and adjusting your goals, and staying committed and persistent. By following this process, you empower yourself to manifest greater wealth, abundance, and prosperity in your life.

- Leveraging the abundance mindset to attract wealth effortlessly

Leveraging the abundance mindset to attract wealth effortlessly involves cultivating a mindset that is focused on abundance rather than scarcity. It entails shifting your beliefs, thoughts, and behaviors to align with the belief that there is more than enough abundance available to you in all areas of life. Here's a comprehensive discussion of the process:

1. **Understanding the Abundance Mindset:** The abundance mindset is a belief system that views the world as abundant and full of opportunities. It is grounded in the belief that there is more than enough wealth, resources, and opportunities to go around for everyone. Individuals with an abundance mindset see setbacks as temporary and believe in their ability to create and attract abundance effortlessly.

2. **Identify and Challenge Scarcity Beliefs:** The first step in leveraging the abundance mindset is to identify and challenge any scarcity beliefs that may be holding you back. These beliefs often stem from childhood conditioning, societal norms, or past experiences of lack. Common scarcity beliefs include "There's not enough to go around," "I'll never be wealthy," or "Money is hard to come by." By recognizing these limiting beliefs and

challenging their validity, you can begin to shift towards an abundance mindset.

3. Cultivate Gratitude and Appreciation: Gratitude is a powerful practice for cultivating an abundance mindset. Take time each day to acknowledge and appreciate the abundance that already exists in your life, whether it be in the form of relationships, opportunities, or simple blessings. By focusing on what you have rather than what you lack, you shift your perspective towards abundance and attract more of it into your life.

4. Visualize Your Desired Outcome: Visualization is a potent tool for manifesting abundance effortlessly. Take time each day to visualize yourself living the life of abundance you desire. Imagine yourself surrounded by wealth, success, and prosperity in vivid detail. Engage all your senses and emotions as you visualize your desired outcome, reinforcing your belief in the abundance that is available to you.

5. **Act As If:** Acting as if you already have the abundance you desire is a powerful way to align your actions with your intentions. Instead of waiting for wealth to come to you, take inspired action as if you are already wealthy. This may involve making financial decisions from a place of abundance, investing in yourself and your goals, and seizing opportunities that come your way with confidence and conviction.

6. **Surround Yourself with Abundance:** Surrounding yourself with people, resources, and environments that embody abundance reinforces your abundance mindset. Associate with individuals who have a positive mindset, immerse yourself in inspirational content and expose yourself to opportunities for growth and success. By surrounding yourself with abundance, you create an energetic environment that supports your efforts to attract wealth effortlessly.

7. **Release Attachment to Outcomes:** Letting go of attachment to specific outcomes is essential for manifesting abundance effortlessly. Trust in the

process and surrender to the universe's timing, knowing that abundance will flow to you in divine timing. Release any feelings of desperation or lack, and instead, cultivate a sense of trust, faith, and gratitude for the abundance that is on its way to you.

8. **Practice Generosity and Giving:** Practicing generosity and giving back to others is a powerful way to align yourself with the flow of abundance. Give freely of your time, resources, and talents, knowing that the more you give, the more you will receive. By cultivating a spirit of generosity, you open yourself up to receiving abundance from unexpected sources and create a positive ripple effect of abundance in the world.

In summary, leveraging the abundance mindset to attract wealth effortlessly involves identifying and challenging scarcity beliefs, cultivating gratitude and appreciation, visualizing your desired outcome, acting as if you already have abundance, surrounding yourself with abundance, releasing attachment to outcomes, and practicing generosity and giving. By adopting these practices and beliefs, you align yourself with the flow of abundance and effortlessly attract wealth, success, and prosperity into your life.

- Exploring practical strategies for wealth creation and financial freedom

Practical strategies for wealth creation and financial freedom involve a combination of earning, saving, investing, and managing money wisely. These strategies aim to build long-term wealth and achieve financial independence. Here's a comprehensive discussion on practical strategies for wealth creation and financial freedom:

1. **Set Clear Financial Goals:** Begin by setting clear and specific financial goals. Determine how much wealth you want to accumulate, by when, and

for what purpose. Your goals may include achieving a certain level of savings, paying off debt, investing in assets, or building passive income streams. Setting clear goals provides direction and motivation for your wealth-building efforts.

2. **Create a Budget and Stick to It:** Develop a detailed budget that outlines your income, expenses, and savings goals. Track your spending habits and identify areas where you can cut back or save more. Allocate a portion of your income towards savings and investments each month, and prioritize paying off high-interest debt. Sticking to a budget helps you live within your means and grow your wealth over time.

3. **Increase Your Income:** Increasing your income is a fundamental aspect of wealth creation. Explore opportunities to boost your earning potential, whether through salary negotiations, career advancement, side hustles, freelance work, or entrepreneurship. Invest in your education and skill development to enhance your earning capacity and open up new avenues for income generation.

4. Save and Invest Consistently: Consistent saving and investing are key to building long-term wealth. Set up automatic transfers to your savings and investment accounts each month to ensure disciplined saving habits. Maximize contributions to tax-advantaged retirement accounts such as 401(k)s, IRAs, and HSAs. Diversify your investment portfolio across asset classes such as stocks, bonds, real estate, and alternative investments to mitigate risk and maximize returns.

5. Live Below Your Means: Adopt a frugal lifestyle and prioritize saving and investing over excessive spending. Avoid lifestyle inflation by resisting the urge to upgrade your lifestyle with every increase in income. Live below your means and embrace a minimalist mindset, focusing on experiences and meaningful purchases rather than material possessions. Redirect saved funds towards wealth-building activities such as debt repayment, investing, and asset acquisition.

6. **Manage Debt Wisely:** Pay off high-interest debt aggressively to reduce financial stress and free up cash flow for wealth-building activities. Prioritize debts with the highest interest rates, such as credit card debt and personal loans, while making minimum payments on lower-interest debts. Consider consolidating high-interest debts or refinancing to lower interest rates and accelerate debt repayment.

7. **Build Multiple Streams of Income:** Diversify your income streams to create resilience and enhance your financial stability. In addition to your primary source of income, explore opportunities to generate passive income through investments, rental properties, dividends, royalties, affiliate marketing, or online businesses. Building multiple streams of income provides additional financial security and accelerates wealth accumulation.

8. **Protect Your Assets and Income:** Safeguard your wealth and financial future by adequately protecting your assets and income. Purchase appropriate insurance coverage, including health

insurance, life insurance, disability insurance, and liability insurance, to mitigate risks and protect against unforeseen events. Establish emergency funds to cover unexpected expenses and financial emergencies, ensuring that you have a safety net in place during challenging times.

9. **Continuously Educate Yourself:** Stay informed about personal finance, investing, and wealth-building strategies by continuously educating yourself. Read books, attend seminars, take online courses, and seek advice from financial experts to expand your knowledge and skills. Stay up-to-date on market trends, economic developments, and regulatory changes that may impact your financial decisions.

10. **Plan for the Long Term**: Adopt a long-term perspective when it comes to wealth creation and financial planning. Focus on building sustainable wealth that can support your lifestyle and goals over the long term. Develop a comprehensive financial plan that addresses your short-term needs, medium-term goals, and long-term aspirations, taking into

account factors such as retirement planning, estate planning, and legacy considerations.

In summary, practical strategies for wealth creation and financial freedom involve setting clear goals, creating a budget, increasing income, saving and investing consistently, living below your means, managing debt wisely, building multiple streams of income, protecting assets and income, continuously educating yourself, and planning for the long term. By implementing these strategies consistently and diligently, you can build wealth, achieve financial independence, and enjoy greater freedom and security in your financial future.

CHAPTER 5:
ABUNDANCE IN ACTION:
CONTRIBUTION AND IMPACT

Welcome to a chapter that explores the transformative power of abundance in action—where wealth extends beyond personal gain to encompass contribution, generosity, and making a positive impact in the world. In this chapter, we delve into how embracing abundance enables individuals to create meaningful change, uplift communities, and leave a lasting legacy of prosperity.

Abundance in action is about harnessing wealth and resources not only for personal fulfillment but also for the betterment of others and the world at large. It is grounded in the belief that true wealth lies not just in what we accumulate but in what we contribute and the impact we make on the lives of others.

In this chapter, we'll explore a range of themes related to abundance in action:

1. **Philanthropy and Giving**: We'll delve into the transformative power of philanthropy and giving, exploring how acts of generosity and compassion can create ripple effects of abundance and change. From charitable donations to volunteerism, we'll discuss the various ways individuals can give back and make a positive difference in their communities and beyond.

2. **Social Entrepreneurship**: We'll explore the growing movement of social entrepreneurship, where business is used as a force for good to address social and environmental challenges. We'll highlight examples of innovative businesses that prioritize purpose over profit and leverage market-driven solutions to create positive social impact.

3. **Impact Investing**: We'll discuss the concept of impact investing, where investors seek financial returns alongside measurable social and environmental outcomes. We'll explore how impact investors can deploy capital to support projects and initiatives that align with their values and contribute to positive change in areas such as sustainable development, renewable energy, and social justice.

4. **Corporate Social Responsibility**: We'll examine the role of corporations in driving positive social change through corporate social responsibility (CSR) initiatives. We'll discuss how companies can integrate social and environmental considerations into their business practices, supply chains, and stakeholder engagements to create shared value for society and stakeholders.

5. **Community Building and Collaboration**: We'll highlight the importance of community building and collaboration in creating abundance in action. We'll explore how individuals and organizations can come together to address common challenges,

leverage collective resources, and create synergistic solutions that benefit the greater good.

6. **Educational Initiatives:** We'll discuss the transformative power of education as a catalyst for social mobility and empowerment. We'll explore initiatives aimed at expanding access to quality education, promoting lifelong learning, and equipping individuals with the knowledge and skills they need to thrive in a rapidly changing world.

7. **Environmental Stewardship**: We'll examine the imperative of environmental stewardship and sustainable resource management in creating abundance for future generations. We'll discuss strategies for promoting environmental conservation, mitigating climate change, and fostering resilience in the face of ecological challenges.

8. **Personal Empowerment and Advocacy**: We'll highlight the role of personal empowerment and advocacy in driving abundance in action. We'll discuss how individuals can use their voices,

platforms, and resources to advocate for social justice, human rights, and equality, amplifying impact and effecting meaningful change.

As we embark on this exploration of abundance in action, I invite you to consider how you can leverage your wealth, resources, and talents to contribute to a world where abundance is shared, opportunities are accessible, and prosperity is sustainable for all. Together, let's harness the power of abundance to create a brighter, more equitable future for generations to come.

- Recognizing abundance as a tool for positive change

Recognizing abundance as a tool for positive change involves shifting one's perspective from scarcity to sufficiency, acknowledging the wealth of resources, opportunities, and blessings available, and harnessing these abundant resources to create meaningful and sustainable change. Here's a comprehensive discussion of the process:

1. **Cultivating an Abundance Mindset:** The first step in recognizing abundance as a tool for positive change is cultivating an abundance mindset. This involves shifting from a mindset of scarcity, which focuses on limitations and lack, to a mindset of abundance, which acknowledges the abundance of resources and possibilities available. Cultivating an abundance mindset involves practicing gratitude, reframing negative thoughts, and focusing on abundance rather than scarcity in all areas of life.

2. **Acknowledging Resources and Opportunities:** Recognizing abundance as a tool for positive change requires acknowledging the wealth of resources and opportunities available. This includes tangible resources such as financial capital, natural resources, and technology, as well as intangible resources such as knowledge, skills, and networks. By recognizing and leveraging these resources, individuals and communities can create positive change in areas such as education, healthcare,

economic development, and environmental sustainability.

3. **Empowering Others:** Recognizing abundance as a tool for positive change involves empowering others to recognize and leverage their abundance. This may involve providing access to education, training, and opportunities for personal and professional development. By empowering others to recognize their abundance and potential, individuals and communities can create a ripple effect of positive change that extends far beyond their immediate sphere of influence.

4. **Collaboration and Partnership:** Creating positive change often requires collaboration and partnership between individuals, organizations, and communities. Recognizing abundance as a tool for positive change involves identifying areas of common interest and working together to leverage collective resources and expertise. By pooling resources, sharing knowledge, and collaborating on shared goals, individuals and organizations can

create more significant and sustainable impacts than they could alone.

5. **Innovation and Creativity:** Recognizing abundance as a tool for positive change involves embracing innovation and creativity in problem-solving. This may involve thinking outside the box, challenging conventional wisdom, and exploring new approaches to addressing social, environmental, and economic challenges. By harnessing the power of innovation and creativity, individuals and organizations can develop innovative solutions that create positive change and drive progress.

6. **Sustainability and Long-Term Impact:** Recognizing abundance as a tool for positive change requires a commitment to sustainability and long-term impact. This involves considering the long-term consequences of actions and decisions and prioritizing solutions that are environmentally sustainable, socially responsible, and economically viable. By focusing on creating lasting change that benefits current and future generations, individuals

and communities can maximize the positive impact of their efforts.

7. **Personal Responsibility and Accountability:** Recognizing abundance as a tool for positive change requires taking personal responsibility and accountability for one's actions and their impact on others and the world. This involves recognizing the power of individual agency and the role that each person plays in shaping the world around them. By taking ownership of their actions and striving to make a positive difference, individuals can harness the power of abundance to create meaningful and lasting change.

In summary, recognizing abundance as a tool for positive change involves cultivating an abundance mindset, acknowledging resources and opportunities, empowering others, fostering collaboration and partnership, embracing innovation and creativity, prioritizing sustainability and long-term impact, and taking personal responsibility and accountability. By recognizing and leveraging abundance in these ways, individuals and communities can create positive change that transforms lives, communities, and the world.

- Aligning personal goals with the greater good of humanity

Aligning personal goals with the greater good of humanity involves identifying individual aspirations, values, and talents that contribute positively to the well-being of society and the world at large. It requires a conscious effort to pursue goals that not only fulfill personal desires but also serve a higher purpose and make a meaningful impact on others. Here's a comprehensive discussion of the process:

1. **Self-Reflection and Clarification of Values:** The process of aligning personal goals with the greater good begins with self-reflection and clarification of values. Take time to introspect and identify what truly matters to you, both personally

and in the context of society. Reflect on your core values, beliefs, and aspirations, and consider how they align with broader societal needs and challenges.

2. **Identifying Personal Strengths and Passions:** Next, identify your strengths, talents, and passions. Reflect on activities and experiences that energize and inspire you, as well as areas where you excel. Consider how you can leverage your unique skills and talents to contribute to the greater good of humanity in meaningful ways.

3. **Understanding the Needs of Humanity:** Gain an understanding of the pressing needs and challenges facing humanity at local, national, and global levels. Educate yourself about social, environmental, and economic issues, and consider how your personal goals and aspirations can address these challenges and make a positive impact.

4. **Setting Altruistic Goals:** Once you have a clear understanding of your values, strengths, and the needs of humanity, set altruistic goals that align

with the greater good. Identify goals that not only fulfil your desires but also contribute to the well-being of others and advance causes that are important to you. Whether it's improving access to education, promoting environmental sustainability, or fostering social justice, set goals that have a positive impact on humanity.

5. **Seeking Alignment with Purpose:** Align your personal goals with a sense of purpose that transcends individual ambition. Consider how your goals contribute to a larger vision of creating a better world for future generations. Connect your aspirations to a broader sense of meaning and purpose that serves the greater good and aligns with your values and passions.

6. **Collaboration and Collective Action:** Recognize that creating positive change often requires collaboration and collective action. Seek opportunities to collaborate with like-minded individuals, organizations, and communities that share your values and goals. By working together towards common objectives, you can amplify your

impact and achieve greater results than you could alone.

7. Measuring Impact and Adjusting Goals: Continuously monitor and evaluate the impact of your goals and actions on the greater good of humanity. Measure your progress towards achieving your altruistic goals and assess the effectiveness of your efforts in creating positive change. Be open to feedback and adjust your goals as needed to ensure they remain aligned with the evolving needs of society.

8. Practicing Ethical Leadership and Responsibility: As you pursue your personal goals aligned with the greater good, prioritize ethical leadership and responsibility. Act with integrity, honesty, and compassion in all your interactions, and consider the ethical implications of your decisions and actions. Take responsibility for the consequences of your choices and strive to make decisions that benefit not only yourself but also the broader community and the planet.

9. **Cultivating a Mindset of Service and Contribution:** Cultivate a mindset of service and contribution as you pursue your goals aligned with the greater good. Recognize that true fulfilment and success come from making a positive impact on others and contributing to the well-being of humanity. Approach your goals with a spirit of generosity, empathy, and compassion, and seek opportunities to uplift and empower those around you.

In summary, aligning personal goals with the greater good of humanity involves self-reflection, identification of personal strengths and passions, understanding the needs of humanity, setting altruistic goals, seeking alignment with purpose, collaboration and collective action, measuring impact and adjusting goals, practicing ethical leadership and responsibility, and cultivating a mindset of service and contribution. By aligning personal aspirations with the broader goals of creating a better world for all, individuals can harness their talents and passions to make a meaningful and lasting impact on humanity.

- Cultivating a spirit of generosity and abundance through contribution

Cultivating a spirit of generosity and abundance through contribution involves fostering a mindset and lifestyle characterized by giving, sharing, and serving others. It entails embracing the belief that there is an abundance of resources, opportunities, and blessings to be shared with others, and actively seeking ways to contribute positively to the well-being of individuals, communities, and society as a whole. Here's a comprehensive discussion of the process:

1. **Shift from Scarcity to Abundance Mindset:** The first step in cultivating a spirit of generosity

and abundance through contribution is to shift from a mindset of scarcity to one of abundance. Instead of viewing resources as finite and limited, adopt the belief that there is more than enough to go around for everyone. Embrace the idea that giving and sharing not only benefit others but also attract more abundance into your own life.

2. **Practice Gratitude:** Cultivate a practice of gratitude to foster a sense of abundance and appreciation for the blessings in your life. Regularly reflect on and acknowledge the abundance of resources, relationships, and opportunities that you have been fortunate to receive. By focusing on what you have rather than what you lack, you cultivate a mindset of abundance that naturally leads to a spirit of generosity and contribution.

3. **Identify Your Gifts and Talents:** Reflect on your unique gifts, talents, and strengths, and consider how you can use them to contribute positively to others. Whether it's through sharing your time, skills, knowledge, or resources, identify

ways in which you can make a meaningful difference in the lives of those around you.

4. **Set Intentions for Contribution:** Set clear intentions for how you want to contribute to the world and the impact you want to make through your generosity. Whether it's supporting a charitable cause, volunteering your time, or helping a friend in need, be intentional about how you choose to give back.

5. **Start Small and Build Momentum:** Begin by making small acts of generosity and contribution a regular part of your daily life. Whether it's offering a kind word, lending a helping hand, or making a modest donation, every act of kindness and generosity counts. As you build momentum and experience the positive impact of your contributions, you'll be inspired to do more and make a greater difference.

6. **Give Freely and Without Expectation:** Cultivate a spirit of generosity that is rooted in giving freely and without expectation of anything in

return. Give from a place of genuine compassion, empathy, and love, without seeking recognition or reward. Trust that your contributions will create positive ripple effects in the lives of others and come back to you in unexpected ways.

7. **Practice Active Listening and Empathy:** Take the time to actively listen to the needs and concerns of others and empathize with their experiences. Seek to understand the challenges they face and the support they need, and consider how you can contribute to alleviating their suffering or improving their circumstances.

8. **Collaborate and Partner with Others:** Recognize that creating positive change often requires collaboration and collective action. Seek opportunities to collaborate and partner with like-minded individuals, organizations, and communities to amplify your impact and address shared challenges more effectively.

9. **Reflect on the Impact of Your Contributions:**
Regularly reflect on the impact of your
contributions and the difference you are making in
the lives of others. Celebrate your successes and
acknowledge the positive changes you have helped
to facilitate. Use these reflections as motivation to
continue cultivating a spirit of generosity and
abundance through contribution.

10. **Inspire and Empower Others:** Be a source of
inspiration and empowerment for others by sharing
your journey of generosity and contribution.
Encourage and support others in their efforts to give
back and make a positive difference in the world.
By leading by example and lifting others, you create
a ripple effect of generosity and abundance that
extends far beyond your actions.

In summary, cultivating a spirit of generosity and
abundance through contribution involves shifting
from a scarcity to an abundance mindset, practicing
gratitude, identifying your gifts and talents, setting
intentions for contribution, starting small and
building momentum, giving freely and without

expectation, practicing active listening and empathy, collaborating and partnering with others, reflecting on the impact of your contributions, and inspiring and empowering others to do the same. By embracing generosity as a way of life and actively seeking opportunities to contribute to the well-being of others, you create a more compassionate, interconnected, and abundant world for all.

CONCLUSION

In conclusion, "Wealth Whisper: Secrets of Abundance" is not just a book; it's a journey—an exploration of the profound principles and practices that unlock the gates to abundance in all aspects of life. Throughout these pages, we've delved into the depths of the human psyche, unraveling the mysteries of mindset, intention, and action, and uncovering the transformative power of abundance consciousness.

From understanding the multidimensional facets of abundance to harnessing the Law of Attraction, from cultivating a mindset of prosperity to embracing gratitude as the gateway to abundance, each chapter has offered valuable insights and practical strategies for manifesting wealth and prosperity effortlessly.

But beyond the accumulation of material riches, "Wealth Whisper" has illuminated a higher truth— that true wealth lies not in what we possess, but in who we become and how we contribute to the greater good. It has reminded us that abundance is not just about what we receive, but about what we give—that generosity, compassion, and service are the true currencies of abundance.

As we reach the final pages of this book, let us carry forth the wisdom and insights we've gained into our daily lives. Let us continue to cultivate a mindset of abundance, set clear intentions and goals aligned with our highest values, and take inspired action towards creating the life of our dreams.

But above all, let us remember that wealth whispers not just of prosperity, but of purpose—that true abundance is found not in the accumulation of possessions, but in the richness of our relationships, the depth of our experiences, and the impact we make on the world around us.

May "Wealth Whisper: Secrets of Abundance" serve as a guiding light on your journey to wealth and fulfillment, and may you continue to listen to the whispers of abundance that echo within your soul, guiding you towards a life of limitless possibility and boundless joy.

www.ingramcontent.com/pod-product-compliance
Lightning Source LLC
Chambersburg PA
CBHW070139260726
48658CB00001B/486